2010

Assessing Cultural Exposure

An Improved Framework for the
Assessment of Cross-Cultural
Exposure Levels in Individuals

By: Todd M. Lowdermilk, MSMIS

Assessing Cultural Exposure
An Improved Framework for the Assessment of
Cross-Cultural Exposure Levels in Individuals

Author: Todd M. Lowdermilk
Editor: Samantha R. Lowdermilk

Cover Art: Amazon Publishing

Initial Project: UMW, June 1st, 2010
First Edition: March 1st, 2012

Library of Congress Control Number (LCCN): 2012904127

ISBN: 1469984512
ISBN-13: 978-1469984513

Printed in the United States of America
Charleston, SC

DEDICATION

I dedicate this publication to my wonderful wife Samantha…

CONTENTS

Todd M. Lowdermilk

ACKNOWLEDGMENTS

This research was conducted as part of a capstone course (MMIS 590) for the Management Information Systems graduate program at the University of Mary Washington. The hope is that someone may pick this up and conduct the study on a larger scale.

I would like to express my gratitude to Virginia Highlands Community College and all of the wonderful professors there. Without community colleges such as VHCC, I would have never been able to accomplish all I have both educationally and professionally. Also, thanks to my brother John for helping motivate me to start college and the rest of my family for encouraging me to succeed.

I would also like to thank my professor, Dr. Mukesh Srivastava for his support and guidance on this research despite the dean's opposition stating that the work was not related to business or information technology. This resulted in a restriction that prohibited the distribution of the assessment to the college student body and other UMW affiliates. This proved to be a severe hindrance by limiting the study to a much smaller sample size than hoped for.

Lastly, I would once again like to thank my wife, Samantha. Not only has she served as the editor of this work, she has also been a tremendous source of motivation for me.

INTRODUCTION

Today's business landscape has undoubtedly evolved into a globalized environment at an unprecedented pace over the last few decades. This is largely due to technical innovation making communications and oversight of cross-cultural business activities both affordable and highly effective. Companies have found that they can dramatically reduce operating costs and increase product-to-market times through the use of properly managed offshore labor. The increased use of the practice has led to some very difficult lessons for companies new to offshoring as they often overlook the importance of the local culture. For purposes of this study, "culture is defined as the socially transmitted behavior patterns, norms, beliefs, and values of a given community" (Vance, Charles M., Yongsun, Paik., 2006). Being insensitive to a locality's culture can at best offend the local workforce, but it has also been known to spell disaster for cross-cultural business activities. This is why cultural intelligence (CQ) becomes important. Being culturally intelligent refers to the individual ability to "understand and act appropriately across a wide range of cultures" (Crowne, Kerri A., 2008). This research is based off Kerri A. Crown's article entitled *"What Leads to Cultural Intelligence"* published by Harvard Business School Publishing. In her article, she established that travel experiences positively contribute to overall cultural intelligence. In this paper, we seek to explain cultural intelligence, define the numerous types of cultural exposures, and develop an assessment to measure their impact on an individual's perceived level of CQ. It was hypothesized that each individual's cultural exposure score as determined by the developed assessment would directly correlate to their perceived level of CQ and that the quality and depth of the various exposures would also add value to the experience. Lastly, the survey was administered to a small random sample which resulted in fifty seven responses. Although the sample size was small, the results were conclusive enough to justify further research on a larger scale.

CULTURAL INTELLIGENCE (CQ)

When the practice of offshoring started to become popular, businesses quickly began to notice that even the most talented employees were sometimes not able to achieve success in managing cross-cultural activities. After closer investigation, they began to realize that part of the problem was due to cultural differences hindering the effectiveness of the business relationship. Such projects were riddled with trust, morale, and communication related issues, many of which were attributed to cultural conflicts. Businesses conducting offshore activities learned that a strong relationship with all entities involved played a big role in any cross-cultural business activity and could dramatically increase the overall odds of success. Sociology has taught us that any action that falls outside a socially accepted norm can be insulting and at the very least make surrounding individuals uncomfortable. Such cultural blunders can seem insignificant but can have a huge impact on the success of a given business activity. For example, refusal of something as simple as a cup of coffee or raising one's voice can be considered insulting or demeaning in some cultures. By assigning an employee to a cross-cultural activity that is well exposed and sensitive to culture, companies can expect higher levels of trust, confidence, effective communications, and increased chances of overall success. It also has the potential to create relationships that allow for new or repeat business endeavors in the future.

A Closer Look

Although an individual can be born with personality traits that naturally make them more culturally intelligent, it is largely something that is gained over time through various cross-cultural exposures. A cultural exposure refers to an "experience related to a region that aids in developing a familiarity with or understanding of the norms, values, and beliefs of the region" (Crowne, Kerri A., 2008). Such experiences can be as simple as watching a foreign TV show or interacting with a foreign coworker. Other more obvious exposures that lead to increased CQ include an individual's level of education, citizenship, and foreign travel experience. Ang Soon, a leading contributor to what is known about CQ, was able to develop a Cultural Intelligence Scale based largely on cultural awareness, sensitivity, and the application of appropriate behaviors. He divided it into four categories representing the four facets of cultural intelligence; this allowed himself and other researchers to pinpoint which factors of CQ are most prevalent in individuals. The four factors of cultural intelligence consist of the meta-cognitive,

cognitive, motivational, and behavioral. Meta-cognitive CQ refers to the way an individual learns and how they interpret or understand information. Cognitive CQ centers upon a person's knowledge of self, their social environment, and their ability to process information. Motivational CQ refers to an individual's desire to learn and function in cross-cultural environments. And lastly, behavioral CQ is a person's willingness to behave appropriately (both verbally and non-verbally) in such cross-cultural environments.

Basis of Research (Gap Identification)

The measure created by Ang Soon is widely accepted but as mentioned, it focuses on cultural awareness, sensitivity, and the ability to apply appropriate behavior. Kerri A. Crown's study leveraged the work of Ang Soon and other researchers to examine the impacts of various cultural exposures on overall CQ in addition to how they affected each of the four facets. Her research focused on citizenship, employment, education, and the number and types of foreign travel experiences. She learned that different types of travel experiences have varying impacts on the four facets of CQ. For example, she was able to conclude that foreign travel for vacation purposes had a positive impact on overall CQ, but the impact was largely motivational. However, it was her second hypothesis in which this research is based. She hypothesized that the quality and depth of a cultural exposure would have a positive impact on an individual's overall level of CQ, but her conclusion was solely based on the number and type of foreign travel occurrences; this did seem to support her hypothesis but was identified as an area for further research. Just as Kerri A. Crowne's research, this study is preliminary and seeks to provide a business tool for the assessment of individuals being considered for foreign work activities.

THE STUDY

Once the gap in available research was identified, the next step was to identify the research questions that would ultimately become the hypotheses for the study. The first question was if an individual's overall level of cultural exposure would correlate with their perceived level of cultural intelligence. Secondly, does the quality of the exposure really add value to the experience? Lastly, do some types of cultural exposures contribute more or less to an individual's level of perceived cultural intelligence? Once the research questions had been identified, a framework of cultural intelligence (Fig 1.0) was created utilizing available research which consolidated known contributors to CQ along with quality aspects (See Appendix) that could be used as a basis for the development of the cultural exposure assessment to be administered later.

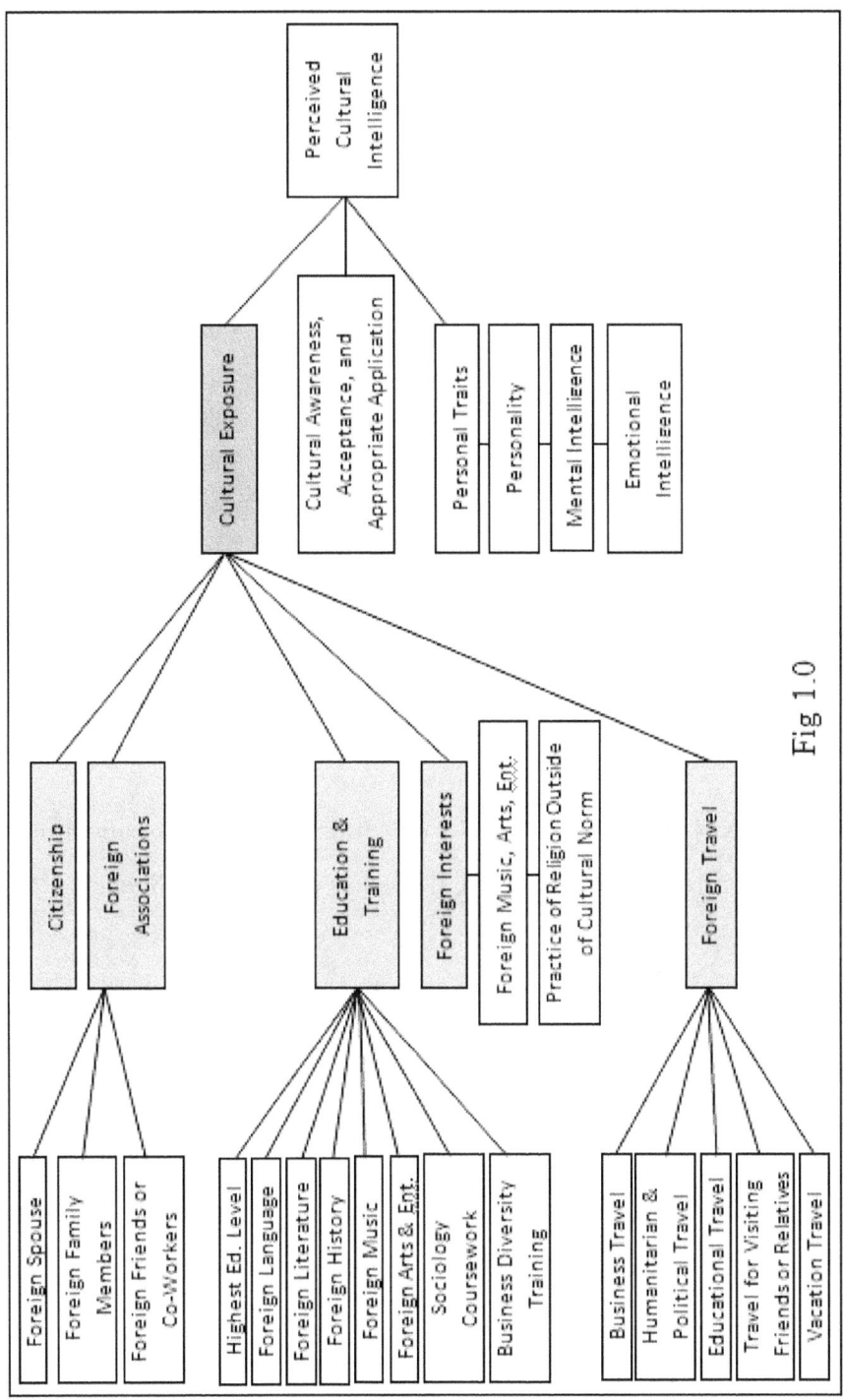

Fig 1.0

Research Methodology and Design

The research framework followed was based on Churchill's Model (See Appendix) (Churchill, Gilbert A., 1979). This iterative methodology utilized a waterfall type process that allowed for survey refinement and provided structured direction that was flexible and allowed for modifications as needed.

The following hypotheses were developed:

H_1. An individual's level of cultural exposure will directly correlate with their perceived level of cultural intelligence.

H_2. The quality and depth of a cultural exposure does add to its value in terms of cultural intelligence.

H_3. An individual's level of cultural exposure will directly correlate with their actual level of cultural intelligence.

Using the previously developed cultural exposure framework, descriptive, dependant and independent variables were identified. The descriptive variable consisted of whether or not the respondent was a member or potential member of the global IT or management workforce. Dependant variables were the respondents perceived level of overall cultural intelligence and their actual level of cultural exposure. The many dimensions or contributors to overall cultural exposure made up the independent variables. An initial assessment was then developed and administered to a small control group for analysis and feedback. The anonymous survey was then refined and administered to an unknown number of individuals through the use of networking and a service called Zarca Interactive, a survey design and data collection service.

Reliability and Validity

To ensure reliability the survey questions were formed from existing research in each perspective area. In areas with limited amounts of information such as the quality aspects of cross-cultural exposures, assumptions were made that the quality measure did add to exposure value. This was later to be validated by a correlation between the quality item and the perceived levels of cultural intelligence. Validity was ensured by protecting the dependant variable results from any manipulation, neutral design of survey items, and the targeted participants were not limited to a specific demographic. The survey resulted in fifty seven respondents which were determined to be adequate for the qualitative preliminary research being conducted.

Assumptions and Limitations

It was initially planned to administer the newly developed Cultural Exposure Assessment (See Appendix) along with Soon Ang's already proven and widely accepted Cultural Intelligence Scale. However, it was determined that doing so would have made the assessment too long. Instead, the study captured respondents perceived level of cultural intelligence. Another limitation was the sample size itself (57 Respondents); this was determined to be adequate given the preliminary nature of the research.

Data Analysis

Due to the small number of respondents the data analysis was deemed to be non-parametric. Each survey item determined to be an independent variable was assigned a numerical weight. Independent variables were grouped into five categories consisting of citizenship, associations, education, foreign interests, and foreign travel experiences. The sum of the weights in each exposure group resulted in a total score for the area of cultural exposure. When all exposure categories were tallied, the result was an overall score reflecting an individual's overall level of cultural exposure. The overall score as well as the category scores could then be compared against the dependant variable, participant levels of perceived cultural intelligence.

RESULTS AND DISCUSSION

Descriptive Statistics

      The distribution of the newly developed Cultural Exposure Assessment resulted in fifty seven responses from varying demographics. Descriptive statistics include the following:

- Current or potential member of the global IT or management workforce
- Perceived level of overall cultural intelligence
- Citizenship status
- Highest education level
- Foreign travel
- Grouped overall cultural exposure score

Of the responses, ten came from individuals who were current or potential future members of the global IT or management workforce. The remaining forty-seven responses were universal participants from varying demographics. Also of high importance, the majority of the respondents perceived themselves as having a moderate or better level of overall CQ.

Perceived CQ

		Frequency	Percent	Valid Percent	Cumulative Percent
Valid	Not at All	6	10.5	10.5	10.5
	1	4	7.0	7.0	17.5
	2	4	7.0	7.0	24.6
	3	7	12.3	12.3	36.8
	Moderate	18	31.6	31.6	68.4
	5	3	5.3	5.3	73.7
	6	7	12.3	12.3	86.0
	7	5	8.8	8.8	94.7
	8	3	5.3	5.3	100.0
	Total	57	100.0	100.0	

Perceived CQ

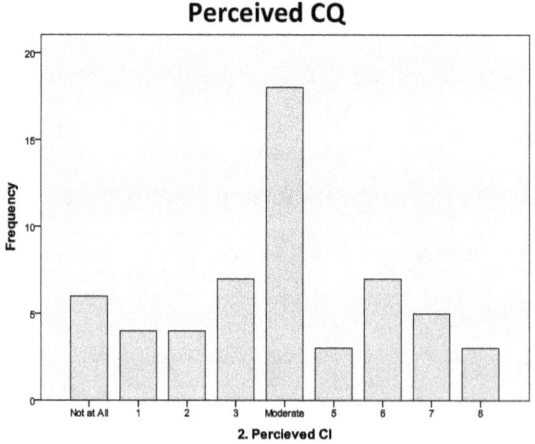

In terms of citizenship, only one survey response came from an individual who was not a native born U.S. Citizen. The majority of individuals taking the assessment also had between two and four years of college education. Fourteen of the survey's participants had never been outside their country of origin with the majority of the remaining participants' foreign travel experiences being less than seven.

Overall Cultural Exposure Scores. The assessment was developed with the overall cultural exposure score in mind. In addition to the overall result, scores among the grouped cultural exposure dimensions could also be evaluated. Each survey question was assigned a numerical weight; this was then tallied inside each perspective group to achieve a group score. The groups consist of citizenship, associations, education, foreign interests, and foreign travel. Once tallied, each group score is totaled to achieve an overall cultural exposure score. The theory is that the higher the score, the more the individual has been exposed to foreign cultures. This project hypothesized that this will directly correlate with an individual's perceived level of cultural intelligence.

> **Citizenship Scores:**

Fifty six of the survey's participants were all native born U.S. Citizens with only one being a naturalized U.S. Citizen. Although Kerri A. Crowne's initial research concluded that U.S. Citizenship positively contributed to overall cultural intelligence, a weight of one point was assigned to being a native born U.S. Citizen. The assumption was that a naturalized U.S. Citizen or Dual Citizen taking the survey would be more culturally intelligent than the typical U.S. Citizen. The results were that fifty-six participants received a score of one, and one participant received a score of twenty four (2 points for not being a native born U.S. Citizen, 1 point for being a naturalized U.S. Citizen, and 21 points representing the number of years they had lived in the United States).

➢ **Foreign Association Scores:**

The maximum score an individual could receive for foreign associations was 4, with the typical participant earning 1 or 2 points. This indicates that the average participant only moderately associated themselves with individuals from foreign cultures.

➢ **Education & Training Scores:**

Education and training scores were obtained by assigning an incremental numerical weight to the highest level of education question and adding that weight to the response of the other yes/no (Yes=1 / No=0) questions in the educational category. The result was a score that heavily reflected a participant's education level with added points for other education or training exposures.

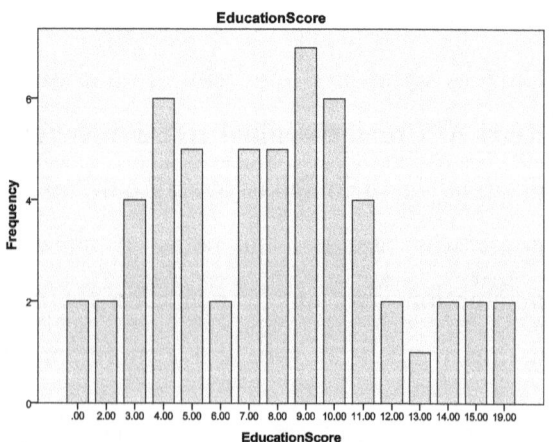

EducationScore		
N	Valid	57
	Missing	0
Median		8.0000
Range		19.00
Minimum		.00
Maximum		19.00

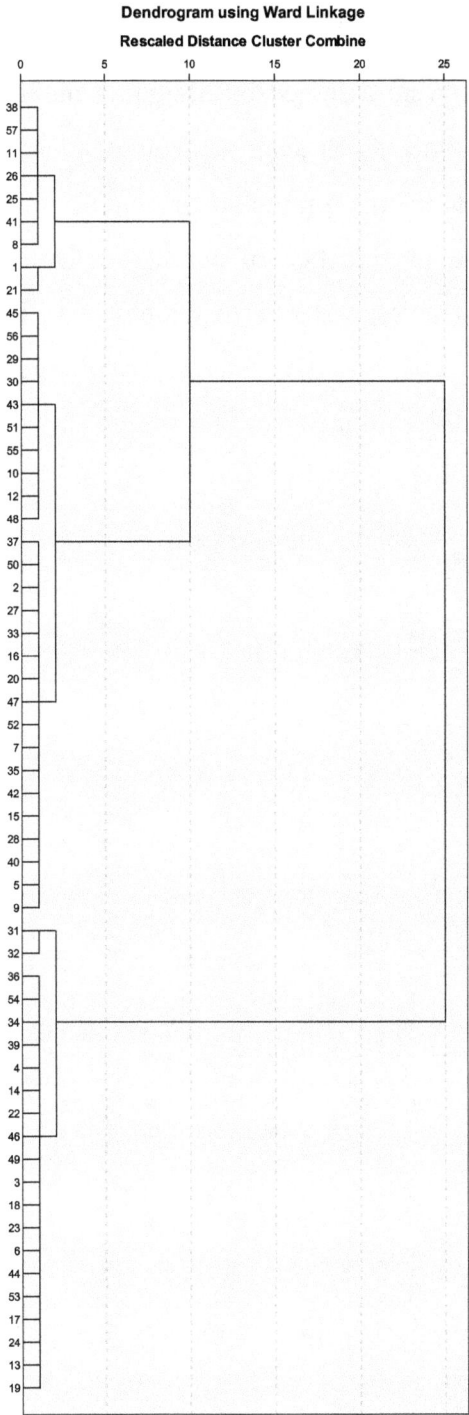

➤ Foreign Interest Scores:

Foreign interests were assessed by assigning numerical weights to foreign interest dimensions such as regular attendance at cultural events, attempts to learn a foreign language outside of an educational environment, and the practice of a religion that falls outside the cultural norm for a respondent's geographic location. The average participant had little to no interest in deliberately exposing themselves to foreign culture.

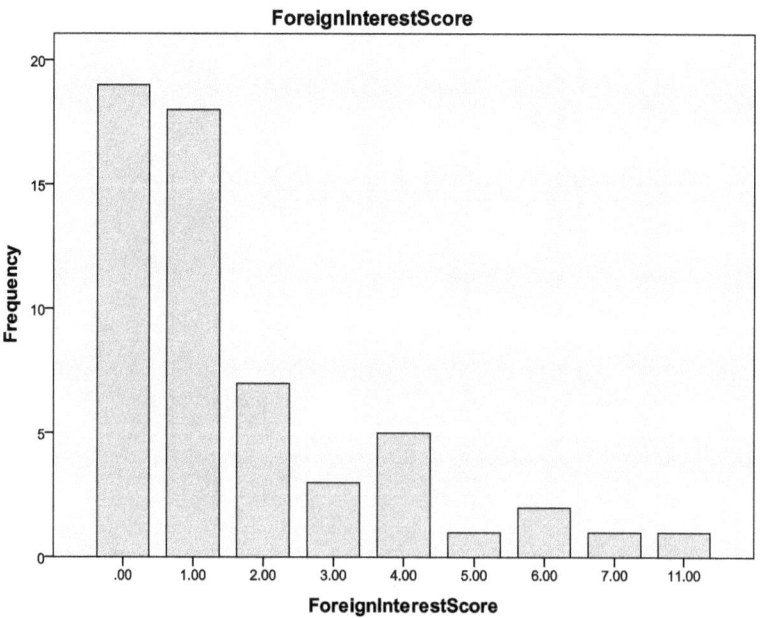

➤ Foreign Travel Scores:

Travel Scores were tabulated by category based on number of travel occurrences, language acquisition, historical knowledge gained, local customs exposure, and level of interaction with the local population. Each item is assigned a weight that was then tallied to provide the travel scores for each category as well as an overall foreign travel score.

Foreign Travel Score Histograms:

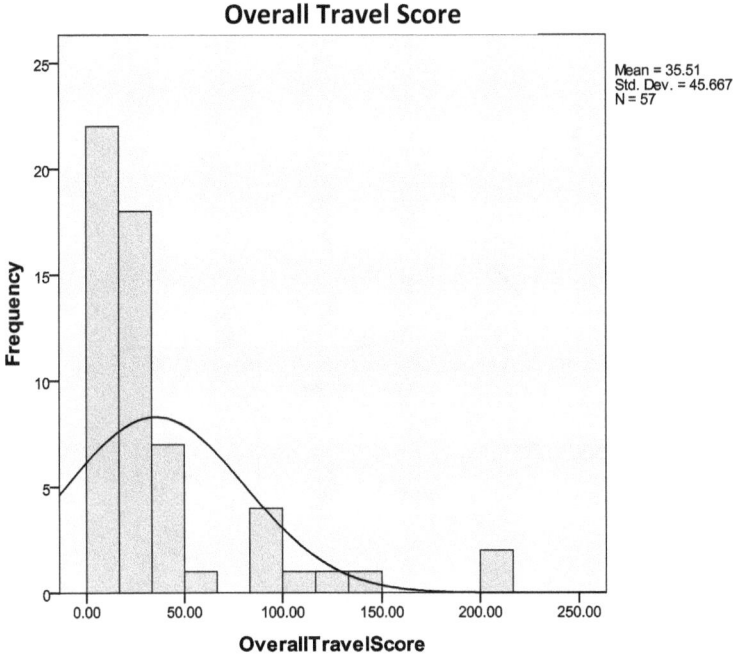

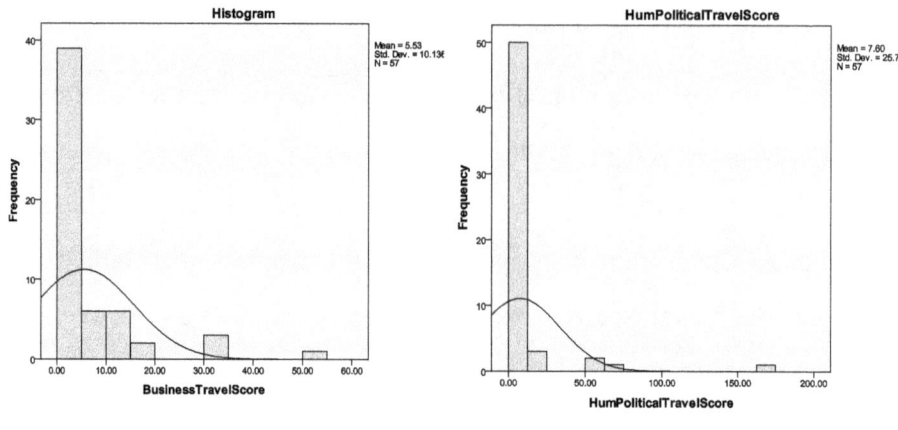

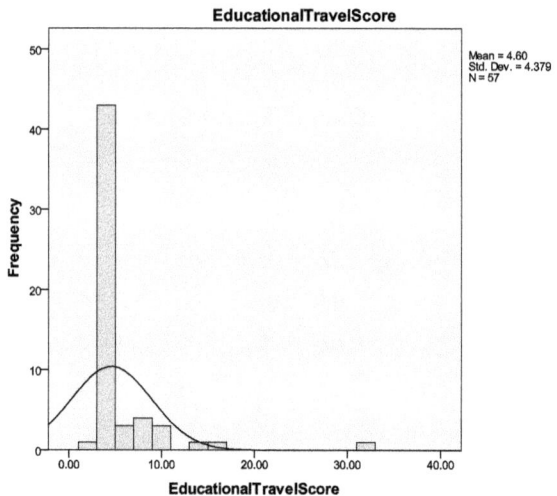

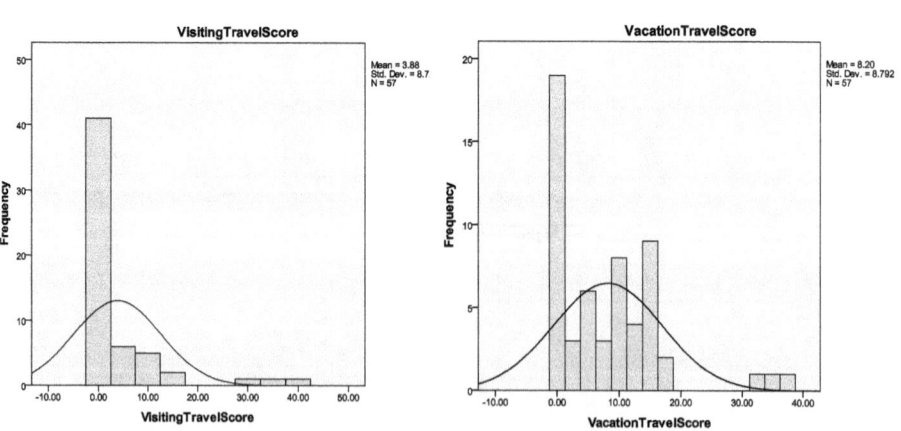

> ## Overall Cultural Exposure Scores:

Of the fifty-seven respondents, the highest score was two hundred and fifty-eight with the median cultural exposure score at thirty-two.

OverallCulturalExposure

		Frequency	Percent	Valid Percent	Cumulative Percent
Valid	6.00	2	3.5	3.5	3.5
	8.00	1	1.8	1.8	5.3
	9.00	2	3.5	3.5	8.8
	11.00	2	3.5	3.5	12.3
	12.00	1	1.8	1.8	14.0
	13.00	2	3.5	3.5	17.5
	15.00	1	1.8	1.8	19.3
	16.00	2	3.5	3.5	22.8
	19.00	4	7.0	7.0	29.8
	20.00	2	3.5	3.5	33.3
	21.00	1	1.8	1.8	35.1
	23.00	1	1.8	1.8	36.8
	25.00	1	1.8	1.8	38.6
	26.00	2	3.5	3.5	42.1
	28.00	1	1.8	1.8	43.9
	30.00	1	1.8	1.8	45.6
	31.00	2	3.5	3.5	49.1
	32.00	1	1.8	1.8	50.9
	33.00	1	1.8	1.8	52.6
	35.00	1	1.8	1.8	54.4
	36.00	2	3.5	3.5	57.9
	37.00	1	1.8	1.8	59.6
	38.00	2	3.5	3.5	63.2
	39.00	1	1.8	1.8	64.9
	40.00	2	3.5	3.5	68.4
	44.00	1	1.8	1.8	70.2
	45.50	1	1.8	1.8	71.9
	55.00	2	3.5	3.5	75.4
	56.00	1	1.8	1.8	77.2
	56.00	1	1.8	1.8	77.2
	58.00	1	1.8	1.8	78.9
	60.00	1	1.8	1.8	80.7
	61.00	1	1.8	1.8	82.5
	68.00	1	1.8	1.8	84.2
	107.30	1	1.8	1.8	86.0
	110.00	1	1.8	1.8	87.7
	113.00	1	1.8	1.8	89.5
	115.00	1	1.8	1.8	91.2
	116.00	1	1.8	1.8	93.0
	132.00	1	1.8	1.8	94.7
	161.00	1	1.8	1.8	96.5
	215.00	1	1.8	1.8	98.2
	258.00	1	1.8	1.8	100.0
	Total	57	100.0	100.0	

Statistics

OverallCulturalExposure

N	Valid	57
	Missing	0
Mean		47.7860
Median		32.0000
Kurtosis		6.213
Std. Error of Kurtosis		.623
Range		258.00
Minimum		.00
Maximum		258.00
Percentiles	25	19.0000
	50	32.0000
	75	55.5000

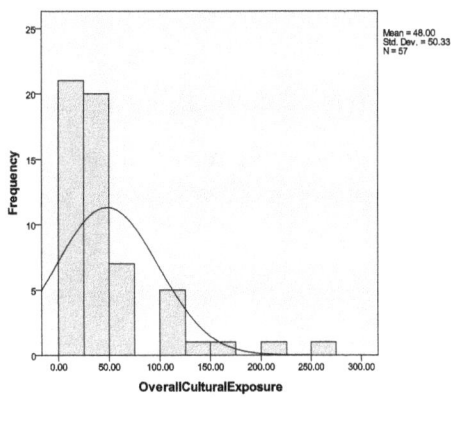

Mean = 48.00
Std. Dev. = 50.33
N = 57

Cultural Exposure Dimensions in Relation to Perceived Cultural Intelligence

Each grouped cultural exposure category (citizenship, associations, education, foreign interests, and foreign travel) was then evaluated in terms of overall perceived level of cultural exposure. In some cases, individual survey items such as membership in the global IT or management workforce, highest level of education, and collegiate level sociology were also analyzed as their results yield surprising results or support previous research in the area. Due to the small sample size (57 participants), the results are preliminary and warrant further investigation and research.

➢ **Member or Potential Member of the Global IT Workforce:** Although the results show that members or potential members of the global IT or management workforce have higher perceptions of their overall cultural intelligence levels, the small sample size yielded less conclusive results than were desired.

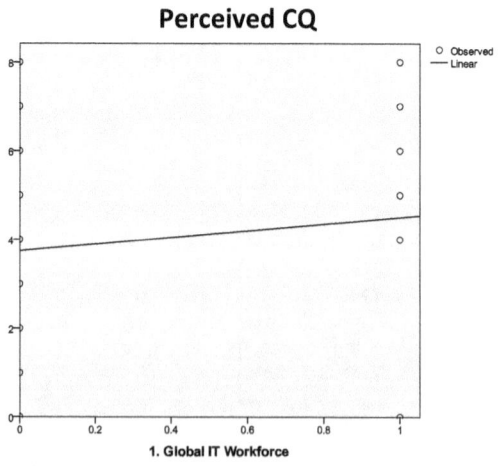

➤ Citizenship:

The results of citizenship in relation to perceived levels of cultural intelligence were also inconclusive due to the small sample size and lack of participants that were not native born U.S. Citizens.

➤ Foreign Associations:

The study suggests that foreign associations such as being married to a foreign spouse, associating with foreign family, friends, or co-workers all lead to higher levels of perceived cultural intelligence which is supported by the results below.

Correlations

			2. Percieved CI	Associations Score
Spearman's rho	2. Percieved CI	Correlation Coefficient	1.000	.121
		Sig. (2-tailed)	.	.369
		N	57	57
	AssociationsScore	Correlation Coefficient	.121	1.000
		Sig. (2-tailed)	.369	.
		N	57	57

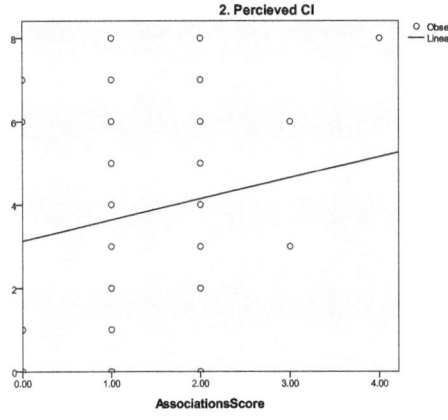

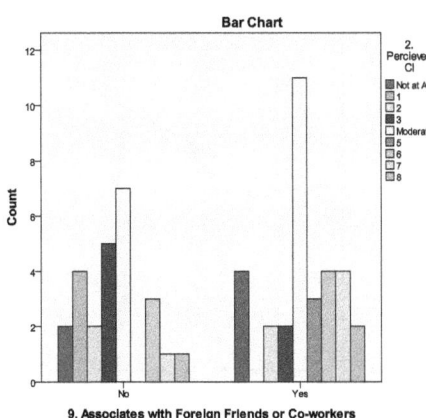

➢ **Education & Training:**

The analysis found that education has a dramatic positive impact on perceived level of cultural intelligence. Despite the small sample size, this result directly supports Kerri A. Crown's findings that an individual's educational level correlates with their overall level of cultural intelligence. This study expanded on her research by also assessing other aspects of education and training such as foreign language, history, literature, arts, and sociology. The surprise result was that even collegiate level sociology has a positive impact on the perceived levels of cultural intelligence in the survey's participants.

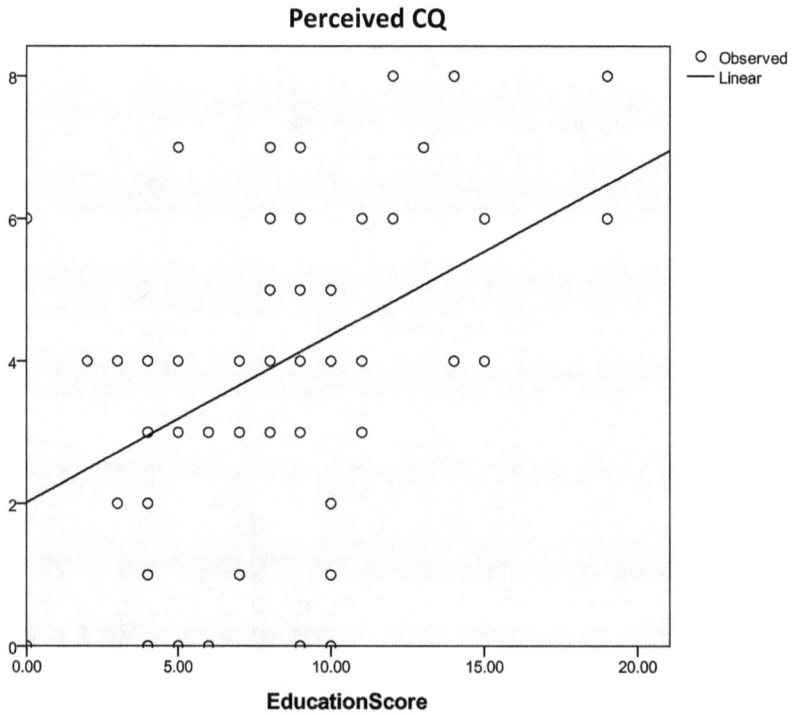

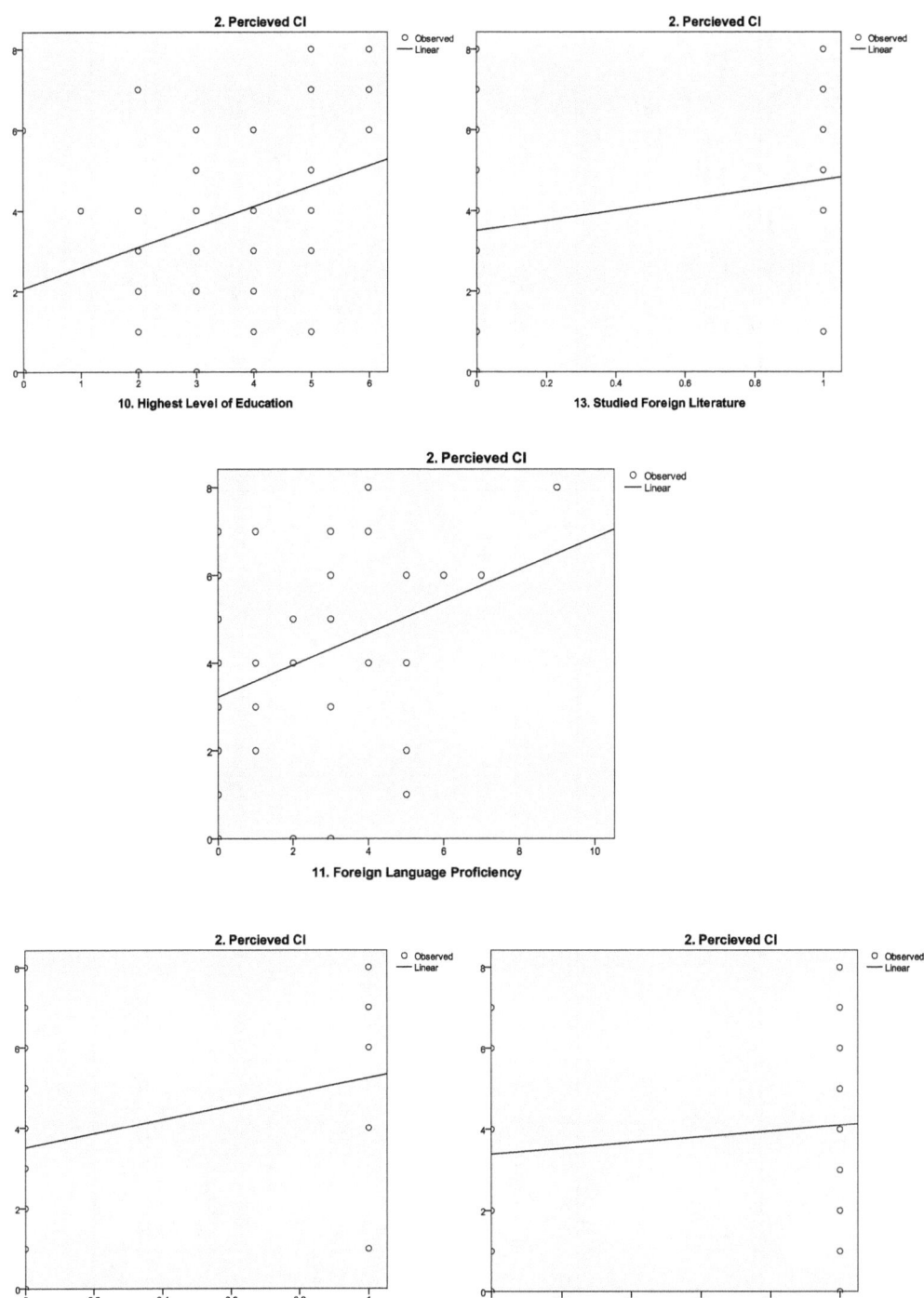

Correlations

		2. Perceived CI	10. Highest Level of Education	11. Foreign Language Proficiency	12. Studied more than 1 Foreign Language	13. Studied Foreign Literature	14. Studied Foreign History	15. Studied Foreign Music	16. Studied Foreign Arts or Entertainment	17. Collegiate Lev. Sociology	18. Participated in Diversity Training
Spearman's rho	2. Perceived CI	Correlation Coefficient	1.000	.334*	.278*	-.080	.302*	.220	.315*	.323*	.132	.211
		Sig. (2-tailed)	.	.011	.036	.555	.023	.100	.017	.014	.327	.114
		N	57	57	57	57	57	57	57	57	57	57
	10. Highest Level of Education	Correlation Coefficient	.334*	1.000	.194	.001	.559**	.302*	.233	.251	.592**	.178
		Sig. (2-tailed)	.011	.	.147	.992	.000	.022	.081	.059	.000	.186
		N	57	57	57	57	57	57	57	57	57	57
	11. Foreign Language Proficiency	Correlation Coefficient	.278*	.194	1.000	.362**	.225	.180	.088	.101	.225	.255
		Sig. (2-tailed)	.036	.147	.	.006	.093	.181	.514	.456	.093	.056
		N	57	57	57	57	57	57	57	57	57	57
	12. Studied more than 1 Foreign Language	Correlation Coefficient	-.080	.001	.362**	1.000	.070	.033	.099	-.143	.045	.237
		Sig. (2-tailed)	.555	.992	.006	.	.605	.806	.465	.287	.738	.076
		N	57	57	57	57	57	57	57	57	57	57
	13. Studied Foreign Literature	Correlation Coefficient	.302*	.559**	.225	.070	1.000	.454**	.361**	.228	.360**	.090
		Sig. (2-tailed)	.023	.000	.093	.605	.	.000	.006	.088	.006	.506
		N	57	57	57	57	57	57	57	57	57	57
	14. Studied Foreign History	Correlation Coefficient	.220	.302*	.180	.033	.454**	1.000	.393**	.431**	.197	.223
		Sig. (2-tailed)	.100	.022	.181	.806	.000	.	.002	.001	.142	.095
		N	57	57	57	57	57	57	57	57	57	57
	15. Studied Foreign Music	Correlation Coefficient	.315*	.233	.088	.099	.361**	.393**	1.000	.293*	.045	.057
		Sig. (2-tailed)	.017	.081	.514	.465	.006	.002	.	.027	.738	.674
		N	57	57	57	57	57	57	57	57	57	57
	16. Studied Foreign Arts or Entertainment	Correlation Coefficient	.323*	.251	.101	-.143	.228	.431**	.293*	1.000	.258	.266*
		Sig. (2-tailed)	.014	.059	.456	.287	.088	.001	.027	.	.052	.045
		N	57	57	57	57	57	57	57	57	57	57
	17. Collegiate Lev. Sociology	Correlation Coefficient	.132	.592**	.225	.045	.360**	.197	.045	.258	1.000	.185
		Sig. (2-tailed)	.327	.000	.093	.738	.006	.142	.738	.052	.	.168
		N	57	57	57	57	57	57	57	57	57	57
	18. Participated in Diversity Training	Correlation Coefficient	.211	.178	.255	.237	.090	.223	.057	.266*	.185	1.000
		Sig. (2-tailed)	.114	.186	.056	.076	.506	.095	.674	.045	.168	.
		N	57	57	57	57	57	57	57	57	57	57

*. Correlation is significant at the 0.05 level (2-tailed).

**. Correlation is significant at the 0.01 level (2-tailed).

> **Foreign Interests:**

Foreign interests also had a positive impact on perceived level of

cultural intelligence with the most predominant factors being

attempts on learning a foreign language outside of a educational

setting and regular attendance at foreign film, arts, or music events.

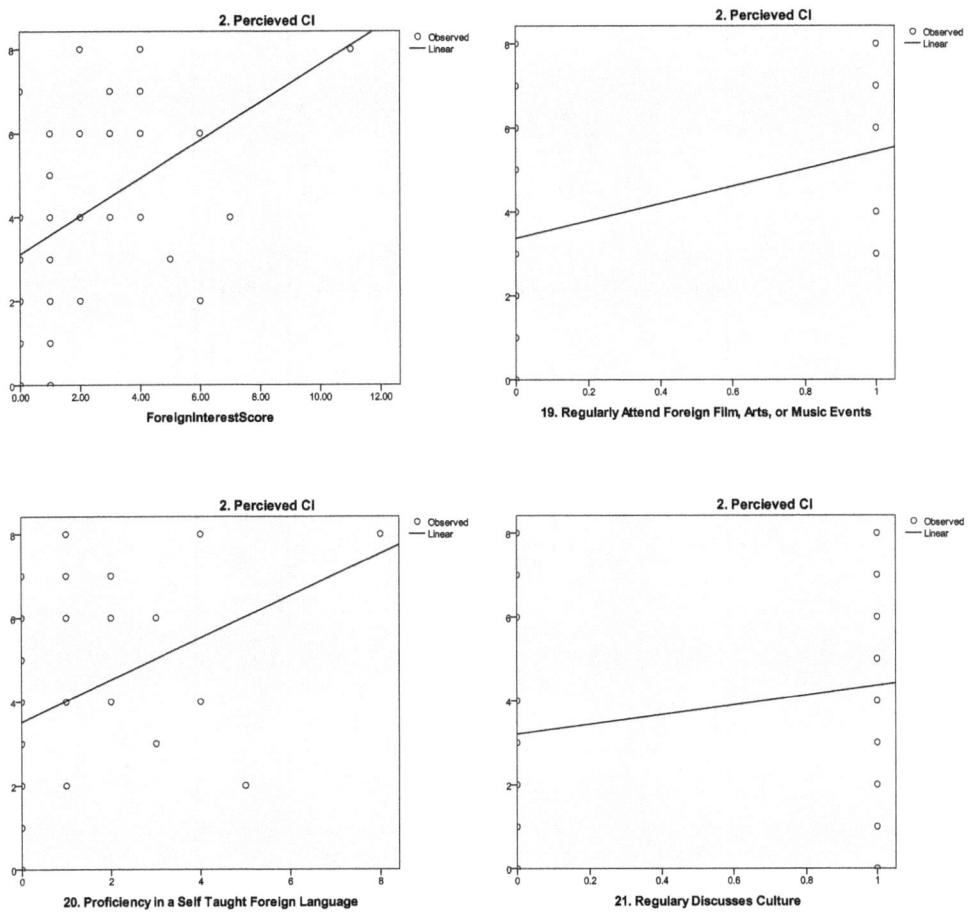

Correlations

		2. Percieved CI	19. Regularly Attend Foreign Film, Arts, or Music Events	20. Proficiency in a Self Taught Foreign Language	21. Regularly Discusses Culture	22. Practices a Religion Outside of Cultural Norm
Spearman's rho	2. Percieved CI					
	Correlation Coefficient	1.000	.384**	.378**	.272*	.313*
	Sig. (2-tailed)	.	.003	.004	.041	.018
	N	57	57	57	57	57
	19. Regularly Attend Foreign Film, Arts, or Music Events					
	Correlation Coefficient	.384**	1.000	.479**	.322*	.356**
	Sig. (2-tailed)	.003	.	.000	.015	.007
	N	57	57	57	57	57
	20. Proficiency in a Self Taught Foreign Language					
	Correlation Coefficient	.378**	.479**	1.000	.304*	.326*
	Sig. (2-tailed)	.004	.000	.	.021	.013
	N	57	57	57	57	57
	21. Regularly Discusses Culture					
	Correlation Coefficient	.272*	.322*	.304*	1.000	.242
	Sig. (2-tailed)	.041	.015	.021	.	.069
	N	57	57	57	57	57
	22. Practices a Religion Outside of Cultural Norm					
	Correlation Coefficient	.313*	.356**	.326*	.242	1.000
	Sig. (2-tailed)	.018	.007	.013	.069	.
	N	57	57	57	57	57

** Correlation is significant at the 0.01 level (2-tailed).

*. Correlation is significant at the 0.05 level (2-tailed).

➤ Foreign Travel:

Kerri A. Crowne's research concluded that the type and quantity of foreign travel had a positive impact on an individual's overall level of cultural intelligence. This research adds a quality element composed of the amount of immersion in the local cultural environment while traveling. The results support Kerri A. Crowne's findings and add that the quality of such travel experiences does contribute to individual perceived levels of cultural intelligence.

Foreign Travel Statistics:

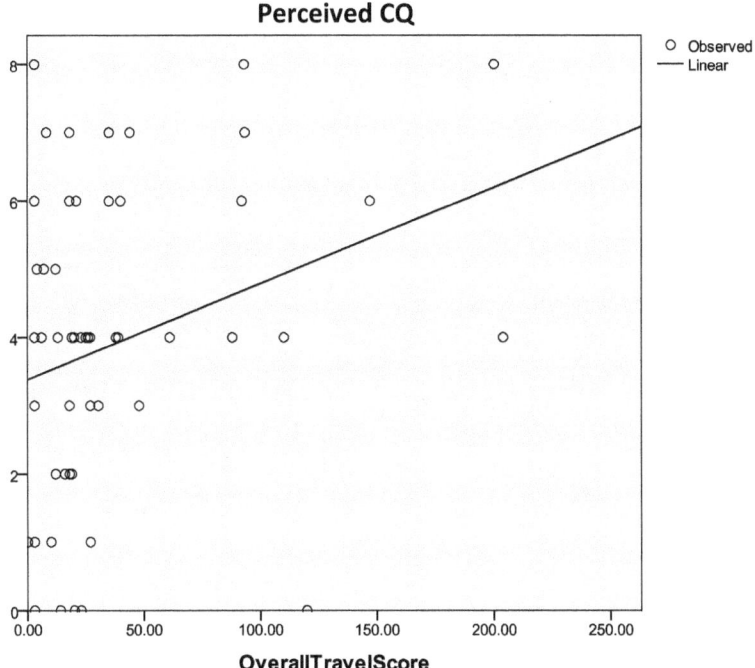

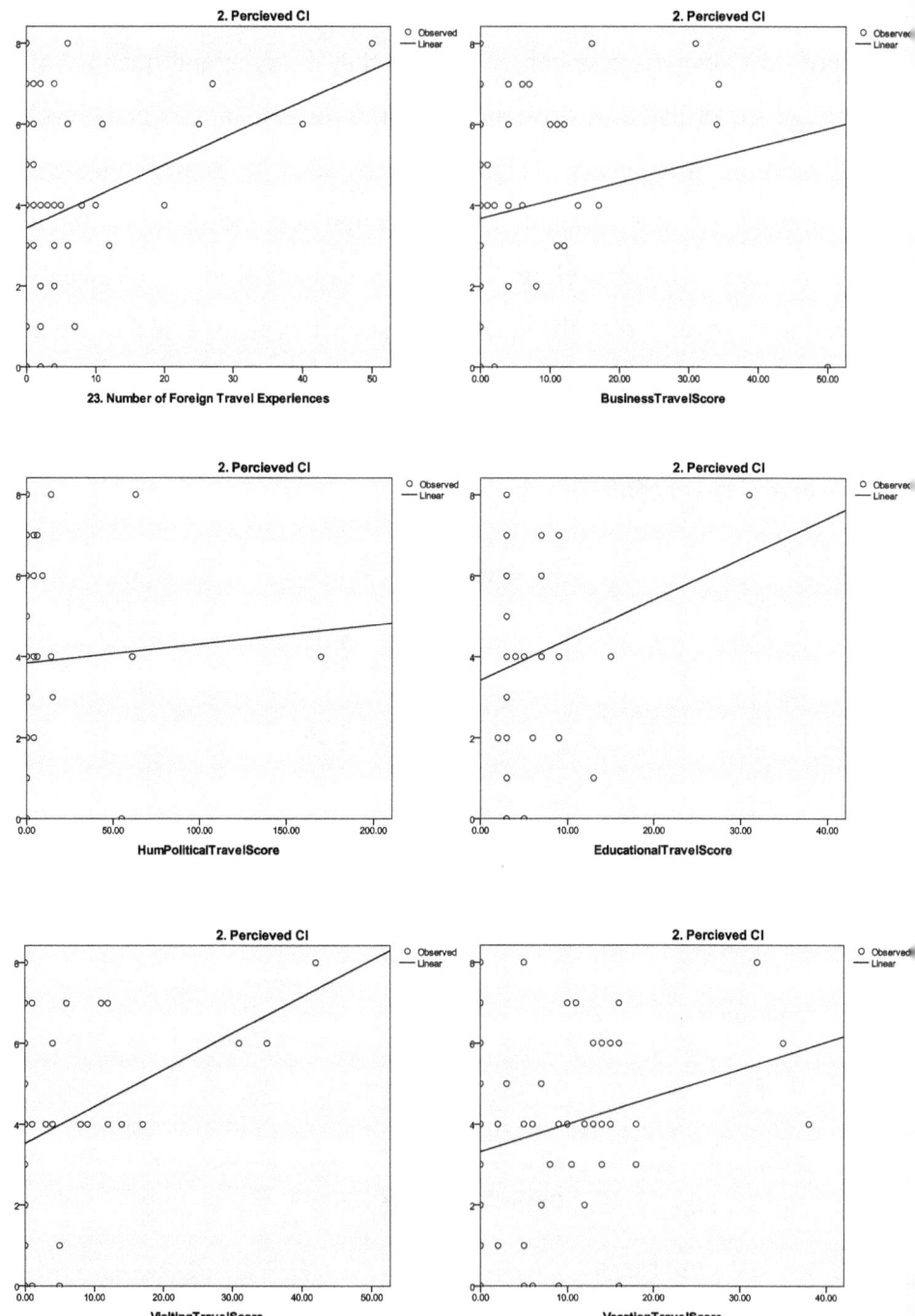

Correlations

		2. Perceived CQ	23. Number of Foreign Travel Experiences	Business TravelScore	HumPolitical TravelScore	Educational TravelScore	VisitingTravel Score	Vacation TravelScore
Spearman's rho	**2. Perceived CQ** Correlation Coefficient	1.000	.159	.349**	.212	.098	.300*	.235
	Sig. (2-tailed)		.237	.008	.113	.467	.024	.078
	N	57	57	56	57	57	57	57
	23. Number of Foreign Travel Experiences Correlation Coefficient	.159	1.000	.530**	.398**	.256	.478**	.668**
	Sig. (2-tailed)	.237		.000	.002	.054	.000	.000
	N	57	57	56	57	57	57	57
	BusinessTravelScore Correlation Coefficient	.349**	.530**	1.000	.504**	.369**	.546**	.218
	Sig. (2-tailed)	.008	.000		.000	.005	.000	.106
	N	56	56	56	56	56	56	56
	HumPoliticalTravelScore Correlation Coefficient	.212	.398**	.504**	1.000	.491**	.488**	.263*
	Sig. (2-tailed)	.113	.002	.000		.000	.000	.048
	N	57	57	56	57	57	57	57
	EducationalTravelScore Correlation Coefficient	.098	.256	.369**	.491**	1.000	.489**	.244
	Sig. (2-tailed)	.467	.054	.005	.000		.000	.067
	N	57	57	56	57	57	57	57
	VisitingTravelScore Correlation Coefficient	.300*	.478**	.546**	.488**	.489**	1.000	.446**
	Sig. (2-tailed)	.024	.000	.000	.000	.000		.001
	N	57	57	56	57	57	57	57
	VacationTravelScore Correlation Coefficient	.235	.668**	.218	.263*	.244	.446**	1.000
	Sig. (2-tailed)	.078	.000	.106	.048	.067	.001	
	N	57	57	56	57	57	57	57

** Correlation is significant at the 0.01 level (2-tailed).

* Correlation is significant at the 0.05 level (2-tailed).

Hypothesis Testing

H₁. An individual's level of cultural exposure will directly correlate with their perceived level of cultural intelligence.

This research does establish that the overall cultural exposure determined by the developed Cultural Exposure Assessment has a direct correlation with perceived levels of overall cultural intelligence.

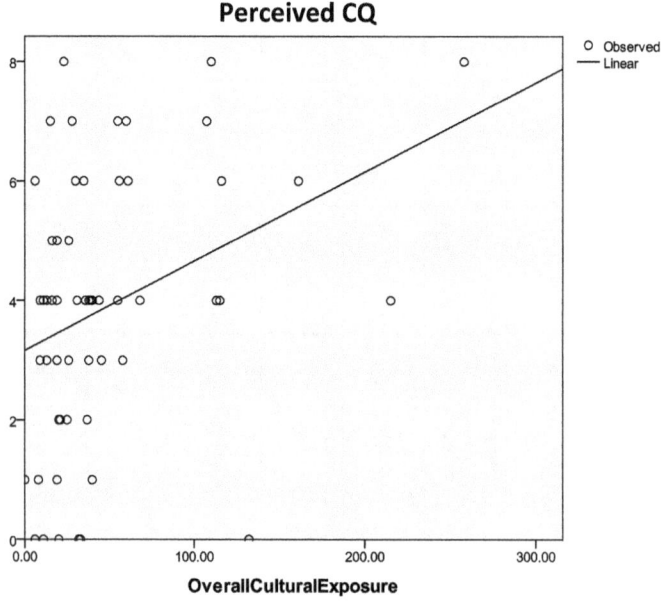

H₂. The quality and depth of a cultural exposure does add to its value in terms of cultural intelligence.

The results of this study support the hypothesis that the quality and depth of a cultural exposure increases the exposure's value in terms of overall cultural intelligence. However, more research is certainly warranted in this area as the developed assessment relied on categorized travel exposures making it difficult to establish a well defined correlation.

See Next Page for Correlations...

Correlations

Spearman's rho		2. Perceived CI	Citizenship Score	Associations Score	Education Score	Foreign Interest Score	Business Travel Score	Hum Political Travel Score	Educational Travel Score	Visiting Travel Score	Vacation Travel Score	Overall Travel Score	Overall Cultural Exposure
2. Perceived CI	Correlation Coefficient	1.000	.224	.121	.418**	.465**	.361**	.212	.098	.300*	.235	.290*	.331*
	Sig. (2-tailed)	.	.095	.369	.001	.000	.006	.113	.467	.024	.078	.029	.012
	N	57	57	57	57	57	57	57	57	57	57	57	57
CitizenshipScore	Correlation Coefficient	.224	1.000	.250	.224	.236	.218	.236	.294*	.271*	.215	.220	.228
	Sig. (2-tailed)	.095	.	.061	.094	.077	.103	.077	.027	.041	.108	.100	.089
	N	57	57	57	57	57	57	57	57	57	57	57	57
AssociationsScore	Correlation Coefficient	.121	.250	1.000	.191	.242	.297*	.270*	.239	.302*	.274*	.307*	.329*
	Sig. (2-tailed)	.369	.061	.	.154	.070	.025	.042	.073	.022	.040	.020	.012
	N	57	57	57	57	57	57	57	57	57	57	57	57
EducationScore	Correlation Coefficient	.418**	.224	.191	1.000	.537**	.436**	.229	.331*	.248	.262*	.376**	.512**
	Sig. (2-tailed)	.001	.094	.154	.	.000	.001	.087	.012	.063	.049	.004	.000
	N	57	57	57	57	57	57	57	57	57	57	57	57
ForeignInterestScore	Correlation Coefficient	.465**	.236	.242	.537**	1.000	.272*	.247	.192	.359**	.418**	.409**	.507**
	Sig. (2-tailed)	.000	.077	.070	.000	.	.040	.064	.153	.006	.001	.002	.000
	N	57	57	57	57	57	57	57	57	57	57	57	57
BusinessTravelScore	Correlation Coefficient	.361**	.218	.297*	.436**	.272*	1.000	.508**	.374**	.552**	.233	.671**	.655**
	Sig. (2-tailed)	.006	.103	.025	.001	.040	.	.000	.004	.000	.081	.000	.000
	N	57	57	57	57	57	57	57	57	57	57	57	57
HumPoliticalTravelScore	Correlation Coefficient	.212	.236	.270*	.229	.247	.508**	1.000	.491**	.488**	.263*	.643**	.635**
	Sig. (2-tailed)	.113	.077	.042	.087	.064	.000	.	.000	.000	.048	.000	.000
	N	57	57	57	57	57	57	57	57	57	57	57	57
EducationalTravelScore	Correlation Coefficient	.098	.294*	.239	.331*	.192	.374**	.491**	1.000	.489**	.244	.428**	.438**
	Sig. (2-tailed)	.467	.027	.073	.012	.153	.004	.000	.	.000	.067	.001	.001
	N	57	57	57	57	57	57	57	57	57	57	57	57
VisitingTravelScore	Correlation Coefficient	.300*	.271*	.302*	.248	.359**	.552**	.488**	.489**	1.000	.446**	.671**	.651**
	Sig. (2-tailed)	.024	.041	.022	.063	.006	.000	.000	.000	.	.001	.000	.000
	N	57	57	57	57	57	57	57	57	57	57	57	57
VacationTravelScore	Correlation Coefficient	.235	.215	.274*	.262*	.418**	.233	.263*	.244	.446**	1.000	.745**	.734**
	Sig. (2-tailed)	.078	.108	.040	.049	.001	.081	.048	.067	.001	.	.000	.000
	N	57	57	57	57	57	57	57	57	57	57	57	57
OverallTravelScore	Correlation Coefficient	.290*	.220	.307*	.376**	.409**	.671**	.643**	.428**	.671**	.745**	1.000	.975**
	Sig. (2-tailed)	.029	.100	.020	.004	.002	.000	.000	.001	.000	.000	.	.000
	N	57	57	57	57	57	57	57	57	57	57	57	57
OverallCulturalExposure	Correlation Coefficient	.331*	.228	.329*	.512**	.507**	.655**	.635**	.438**	.651**	.734**	.975**	1.000
	Sig. (2-tailed)	.012	.089	.012	.000	.000	.000	.000	.001	.000	.000	.000	.
	N	57	57	57	57	57	57	57	57	57	57	57	57

** Correlation is significant at the 0.01 level (2-tailed).

* Correlation is significant at the 0.05 level (2-tailed).

H₃. An individual's level of cultural exposure will directly correlate with their actual level of cultural intelligence.

This hypothesis has not been tested but all indications are that there will be a direct link between overall level of cultural exposure and overall level of cultural intelligence. This statement is largely based on previous research by Soon Ang and Kerri A. Crowne.

CONCLUSION

The study utilized qualitative analysis to determine a correlation between individual levels of cultural exposure and their overall perceived level of cultural intelligence. The sample's descriptive statistics revealed that a majority of the study's participants were native born U.S. Citizens, were not current or potential members of the global IT workforce, had at least a two year college education, had traveled outside of their native country less than five times, and perceived themselves as being moderately culturally intelligent. Although the sample size only consisted of fifty seven participants, the results were still conclusive enough to warrant research on a larger scale. The results support the primary hypothesis that an individual's overall level of cultural exposure does directly correlate with their perceived levels of overall cultural intelligence. This was based on the development of an assessment tool which assigned scores to cultural exposure dimensions taking the quality and depth of many types of such exposures into account.

Although prior research had touched on the quality and depth of cultural exposures being important, significant research that combined all the exposure types and attempted to score their quality could not be found. Along with this result, this study has produced a detailed cultural intelligence framework and an exposure assessment that can be expanded on and refined by future research.

Business Application

Research on Cultural Intelligence (CQ) is of major importance to organizations that conduct business across cultural boundaries as it has been proven time and time again that cultural differences can have a major impact on the success or failure of a given project. The more that is known about what makes one individual more culturally intelligent than another can allow organizations to assess employee levels of CQ helping to ensure that the best workers are assigned to cross-cultural work environments. Not only that, organizations can also use such research to develop training programs that would allow for the cultivation of a culturally intelligent workforce. Such a program would undoubtedly give a company a distinct advantage over their competitors; a welcome feat in today's rapidly evolving global business environment.

APPENDIX

I have included supplemental documentation that should be of use to anyone that seeks to continue work in this area...

    I.   Churchill's Research Model

    II.   Literature Review Matrix

    III. Cultural Exposure Framework

    IV. Detailed Variable Framework

    V.   Cultural Exposure Assessment

I. Churchill's Research Model:

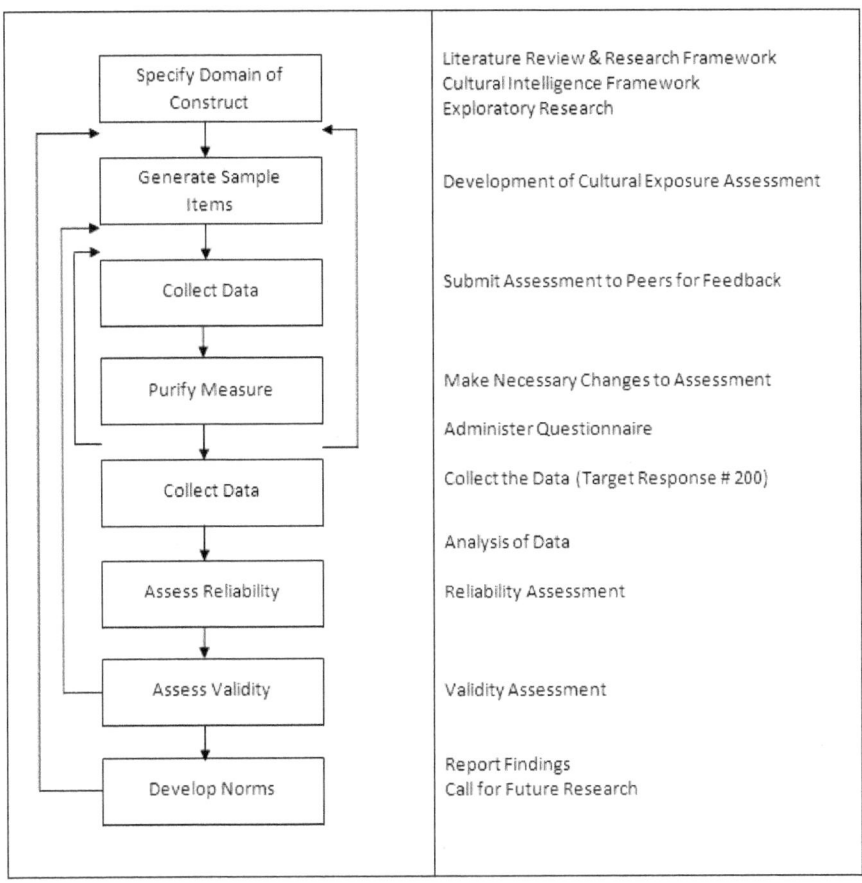

(Churchill, Gilbert A., 1979)

II. Literature Review:

General Topic	Resource
Research Methodology	Churchill, Gilbert A. (1979)
Culture	Caramel, Erran., Tija, Pail. (2005)
Importance of Culture	Caramel, Erran., Tija, Pail. (2005) Brannen, M; Garcia, D; Thomas, D. (February 2009)
General Cultural Intelligence	Ang, Soon; Van Dyne, Linn. (2008) Ang, Soon, Inkpen, Andrew C. (Aug. 2008) Ang, Soon; Van Dyne, Linn; Koh, C.; et al. (2007) Gupta, S. R. (2009) Industry Week. (2009) Koh, C.; Joseph, D.; Ang, S. (February 2009) Li-Rong Lilly Cheng. (2007) Plum, Elisabeth. (February 2004) Sawhney, Teenna. (Dec. 2008) Wilson, Jill. (2007)
Four Factors of Cultural Intelligence	Ang, Soon; Van Dyne, Linn. (2008) Ang, Soon, Inkpen, Andrew C. (Aug. 2008) Crowne, Kerri A. (2008) Messarra, L; Karkoulian, S; Younes, A. (2008)
General Cultural Exposure	Ang, Soon; Van Dyne, Linn. (2008) Ang, Soon, Inkpen, Andrew C. (Aug. 2008) Brannen; Garcia; Thomas. (February 2009) Crowne, Kerri A. (2008)
Measurement of Cultural Intelligence	Ang, Soon; Van Dyne, Linn. (2008) Ang, Soon; Earley, Christopher P. (2003) Ang, Soon; Van Dyne, Linn; Koh, C.; et al. (2007) Crowne, Kerri A. (2008) Cultural Intelligence Center, LLC. (n.d.) Messarra, L; Karkoulian, S; Younes, A. (2008) Swami, Viren; et al. (March 2008)

Acquiring Cultural Intelligence	Messarra, L; Karkoulian, S; Younes, A. (2008) Rabotin, M. (2009).
Contributors/Dimensions of/to Cultural Exposure	**Resource**
Citizenship	Crowne, Kerri A. (2008)
Current Employment	Crowne, Kerri A. (2008)
Number of Cross-Cultural Exposures	Crowne, Kerri A. (2008)
Type of Exposures: Visiting Relatives Vacation Education Employment Living Abroad	Ang, Soon; Van Dyne, Linn. (2008) Ang, Soon, Inkpen, Andrew C. (Aug. 2008) Crowne, Kerri A. (2008)
Length of Exposures	Crowne, Kerri A. (2008)
Personality	Ang, Soon; Van Dyne, Linn. (2008) Kumar, Naresh; Rose, Raduan Che.(2008)
Highest Level of Education	Ang, Soon; Van Dyne, Linn. (2008) Ang, Soon, Inkpen, Andrew C. (Aug. 2008) Crowne, Kerri A. (2008)
Marital Status & Family Cultural Background	
Language Learned	Peltokorpi, V & Schneider, S. (February 2009)
Historical Knowledge Gained	
Exposure to Local Customs	Peltokorpi, V & Schneider, S. (February 2009)
Level of Interaction w/ Foreign Population	
Cross-Cultural Interactions (Family/Friends/Co-workers)	Crowne, Kerri A. (2008)
Foreign Interest (Language/Music/TV)	Crowne, Kerri A. (2008)
Formal Education (Foreign Language Study / Foreign Literature or Historical Study)	Peltokorpi, V & Schneider, S. (February 2009)

Cultural Awareness, Acceptance, and Application	Ang, Soon; Van Dyne, Linn. (2008)
	Ang, Soon, Inkpen, Andrew C. (Aug. 2008)
	Cultural Intelligence Center, LLC. (n.d.)
Miscellaneous	Alon, Ilan; Higgins, James M. (2005)
	Brannen; Garcia; Thomas. (February 2009)
	Caramel, Erran., Tija, Pail. (2005)
	Clausen; Zolner ; Soderberg; Worm. (February 2009)
	Feldt, L. & Jakobsen, M. (February 2009)
	Heckman, Lucy.(2004).
	Holmes, Andrew. (2002)
	Industry Week. (2009)
	Joo-seng Tan. (2004)
	Publishers Weekly. (2008).
	Vance, Charles M., Yongsun, Paik. (2006)

III. Cultural Exposure Framework:

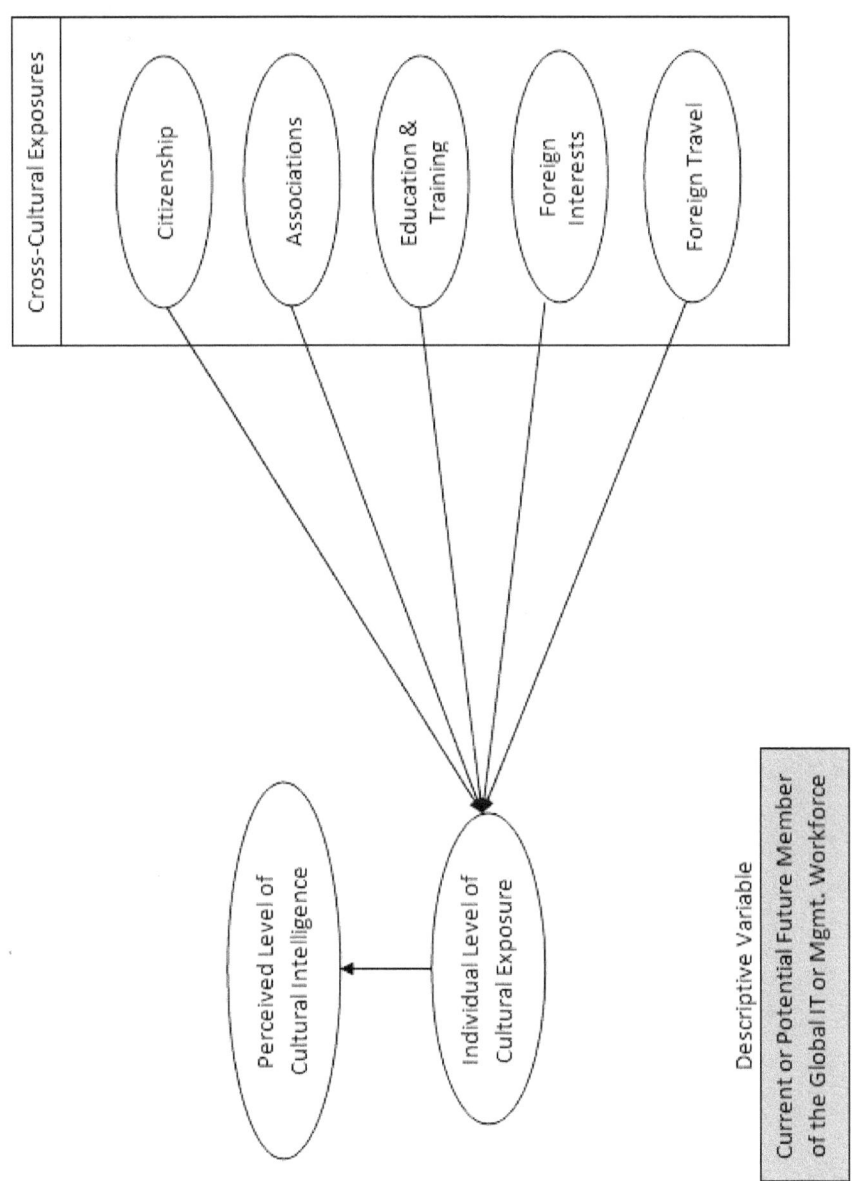

IV. Detailed Variable Framework:

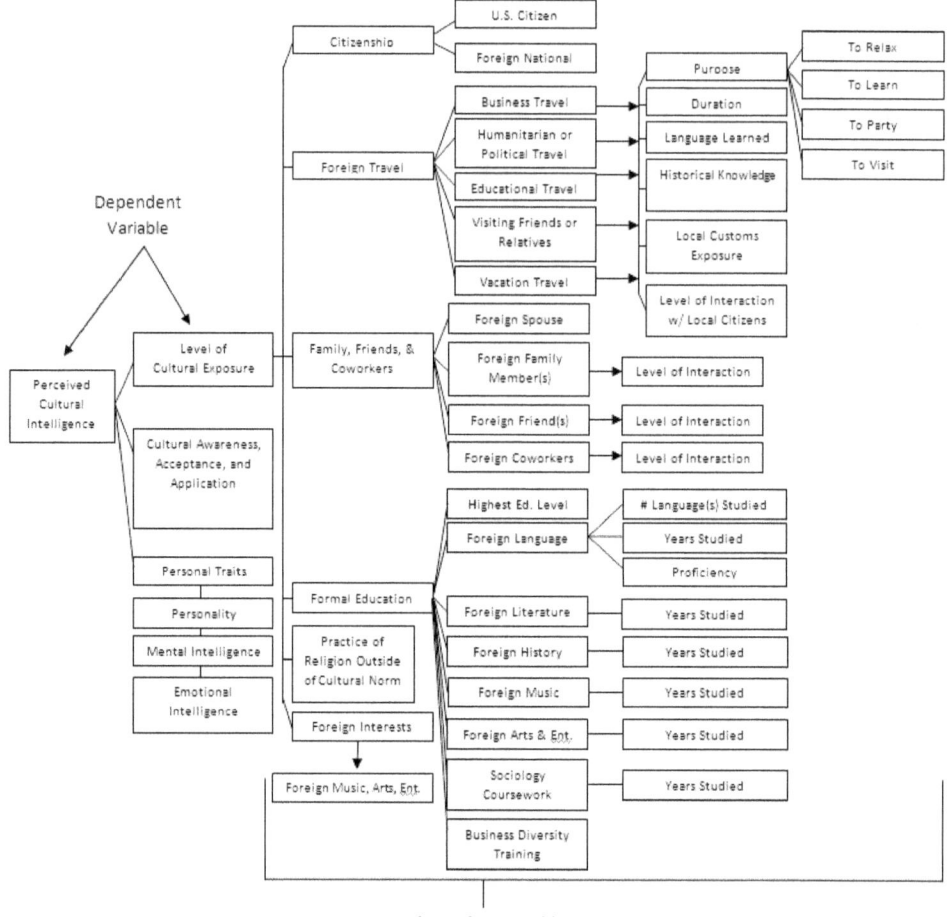

V. Cultural Exposure Assessment:

Cultural Exposure Assessment

1.	Are you a participant or potential participant in the IT Global Workforce or Global Workforce management?	Yes =1	No=0

Section 1: Cultural Intelligence

2.	On a scale from 1 to 10, how culturally intelligent do you think you are? ** Cultural Intelligence is defined as the ability to act appropriately across a wide range of various foreign cultures.* *** 1 = Not at All / 5 = Medium / 9 = Completely*	0 1 2 3 4 5 6 7 8 9

Section 2: Citizenship

3.	Are you a native born United States Citizen? ** A native born U.S. Citizen is one who is born here in the United States.*	Yes =1	No=2
4.	Do you currently hold dual citizenship between the U.S. and another country? ** Dual citizenship means an individual is a citizen of two countries at the same time.*	Yes =1	No=0
5.	Are you a naturalized U.S. Citizen? ** A naturalized U.S. Citizen is a foreign national that has been granted citizenship in the United States after fulfilling certain requirements.*	Yes=1	No=0
6.	If you are a foreign national, how long have you been in the United States? ** A citizen of a country other than the United States.*		_____ Years

Section 3: Associations

7.	If married, is your spouse originally from the United States?	Yes =1	No=2 N/A=0

| 8. | Do you have any family members that are not originally from the United States with whom you regularly associate? | Yes=1 | No=0 |
| 9. | Do you have any friends or co-workers that are not originally from the United States in with whom you regularly associate? | Yes=1 | No=0 |

Section 4: Education & Training

10.	What is your highest level of education?	0	Some School
		1	High School Graduate
		2	Some College
		3	2 Yr. College
		4	4 Yr. College
		5	Post Graduate
		6	Doctorial

11. On a scale from 1 to 10, if you took a foreign language during your education, how would you rate your proficiency?
If you have more than one language then rate the one in which you are most proficient.
** 1 = Minimal / 5= Medium / 9 = Fluent

0 1 2 3 4 5 6 7 8 9

12.	Did you study more than 1 foreign language during your education?	Yes=1	No=0
13.	Did you study foreign literature during college?	Yes=1	No=0
14.	Did you study foreign history in college?	Yes=1	No=0
15.	Did you study foreign music in college?	Yes=1	No=0

16.	Did you study foreign arts or entertainment while in college?	Yes=1	No=0
17.	Have you taken any collegiate level sociology courses?	Yes=1	No=0
18.	Have you participated in any diversity or sensitivity related training?	Yes=1	No=0

Section 5: Foreign Interests

19.	Do you regularly attend foreign film, arts, or music events? ** Regularly is described as more than 3 times in the last year.*	Yes =1	No=0
20.	Have you attempted to learn a foreign language outside of an educational setting; if so, please rate your proficiency in the language on a scale of 1 to 10? ** If you have more than one language then rate the one in which you are most proficient.* *** 1 = Minimal / 5= Medium / 9 = Fluent*	0 1 2 3 4 5 6 7 8 9	
21.	Do you regularly engage in cultural discussions with family, friends, or co-workers? ** Regularly would mean more than 3 times in the past 6 months.* *** Such discussions could be about foreign behavior, politics, arts, language, etc...*	Yes=1	No=0
22.	Do you practice a religion that is outside the cultural norm for your country of origin? ** An example of this would be a practicing Buddhist in a predominantly protestant country.*	Yes=1	No=0

Section 6: Foreign Travel

23. How many times have you traveled outside of your country of origin? _____

24. How many of the above travel occasions were for business? _____
    a. What was the average period of stay during your business travels? _____
    b. Do you typically pick up on any of the local language?   Yes=1   No=0
    c. Did you typically gain any historical knowledge?   Yes=1   No=0
    d. Do you typically expose yourself to the local customs?   Yes=1   No=0
    e. How would you describe your average level of interaction with the local citizens?   0 1 2 3 4 5 6 7 8 9
       * 1 = Minimal / 5=Medium / 9 = Fully Immersed

25. How many of the above travel occasions were for political or humanitarian reasons? (This includes military service) _____
    a. What was the average period of stay during your travels for political or humanitarian reasons? _____
    b. Do you typically pick up on any of the local language?   Yes=1   No=0
    c. Did you typically gain any historical knowledge?   Yes=1   No=0
    d. Do you typically expose yourself to the local customs?   Yes=1   No=0
    e. How would you describe your average level of interaction with the local citizens?   1 2 3 4 5 6 7 8 9 10   0 1 2 3 4 5 6 7 8 9
       * 1 = Minimal / 5=Medium / 9 = Fully Immersed

26. How many of the above travel occasions were for education?   _____

    f.   What was the average period of stay during your educational travels?   _____

    g.   Do you typically pick up on any of the local language?   Yes=1   No=0

    h.   Did you typically gain any historical knowledge?   Yes=1   No=0

    i.   Do you typically expose yourself to the local customs?   Yes=1   No=0

    j.   How would you describe your average level of interaction with the local citizens?   0 1 2 3 4 5 6 7 8 9
        1 = Minimal / 5=Medium / 9 = Fully Immersed

27. How many of the above travel occasions were for visiting friends or relatives?   _____

    a.   What was the average period of stay during your travels for visiting with friends or relatives?   _____

    b.   Do you typically pick up on any of the local language?   Yes=1   No=0

    c.   Did you typically gain any historical knowledge?   Yes=1   No=0

    d.   Do you typically expose yourself to the local customs?   Yes=1   No=0

    e.   How would you describe your average level of interaction with the local citizens?   0 1 2 3 4 5 6 7 8 9
        1 = Minimal / 5=Medium / 9 = Fully Immersed

28. How many of the above travel occasions were for vacation? _____

    a. What was the average period of stay during your travels for vacation? _____

    b. Do you typically pick up on any of the local language? Yes=1 No=0

    c. Did you typically gain any historical knowledge? Yes=1 No=0

    d. Do you typically expose yourself to the local customs? Yes=1 No=0

    e. How would you describe your average level of interaction with the local citizens? 0 1 2 3 4 5 6 7 8 9

       1 = Minimal / 5=Medium / 9 = Fully Immersed

REFERENCES

Alon, Ilan; Higgins, James M. (2005). Global leadership success through emotional and cultural Intelligences, *Business Horizons, (Nov/Dec2005, Vol. 48 Issue 6, p501-512, 12p)*. Retrieved from: UMW Library Resources (Computers & Applied Sciences Complete), December 08, 2009.

Ang, Soon; Earley, Christopher P. (2003). Cultural Intelligence: Individual Interactions across Cultures. Stanford, CA: Stanford University Press

Ang, Soon, Inkpen, Andrew C. (Aug. 2008), Cultural Intelligence and Offshore Outsourcing Success: A Framework of Firm-Level Intercultural Capability, *Decision Sciences, (Aug2008, Vol. 39 Issue 3, p337-358, 22p)*. Retrieved from: UMW Library Resources (Business Source Complete), May 23, 2009.

Ang, Soon; Van Dyne, Linn. (2008). Handbook of Cultural Intelligence: Theory, Measurement, and Application. Armonk, NY: M.E. Sharpe, Inc.

Ang, Soon; Van Dyne, Linn; Koh, Christine; Ng, K. Yee; Templer, Klaus J.; Tay, Cheryl; Chandrasekar, N. Anand.(2007). Cultural Intelligence: Its Measurement and Effects on Cultural Judgment and Decision Making, Cultural Adaptation and Task Performance, Management & Organization Review, (Nov. 2007, Vol. 3, Issue 3, p335-371, 37p). Retrieved from: UMW Library Resources (Business Source Complete), May 23, 2009.

Brannen, Mary Yoko; Garcia, Dominie; Thomas, David C. (February 2009). Biculturals as natural bridges for intercultural communication and collaboration, *ACM, (Feb2009, IWIC '09: Proceeding of the 2009 international workshop on Intercultural collaboration)*. Retrieved from: UMW Library Resources (The ACM Digital Library), December 08, 2009.

Caramel, Erran., Tija, Pail. (2005). Offshoring Information Technology: Sourcing and Outsourcing to a Global Workforce. Cambridge University Press.

Churchill, Gilbert A. (1979). A Paradigm for Developing Better Measures of Marketing Constructs. Journal of Marketing Research, (Feb. 1979, 16:1, p64-73, 10p). Retrived From:http://www.mona.uwi.edu/dmcs/staff/gmansingh/Resea rch%20Methods/Quantitative%20Methods/Chruchill-JMR-16-1.pdf on December 13, 2009

Clausen, Lisbeth; Zolner, Mette; Soderberg, Anne-Marie; Worm, Verner. (February 2009). Cultural intelligence as a strategic resource in multicultural teams, *ACM, (Feb2009, IWIC '09: Proceeding of the 2009 international workshop on Intercultural collaboration)*. Retrieved from: UMW Library Resources (The ACM Digital Library), December 08, 2009.

Crowne, Kerri A. (2008). What Leads to Cultural Intelligence. *(Harvard Business School Publishing)*. Retrieved May 20, 2009 from: UMW Blackboard Site (MMIS 531)

Cultural Intelligence Center, LLC. (n.d.) General Cultural Intelligence Information and Measurement, Retrieved from: www. culturalq.com, December 12, 2009

Gupta, S. R. (2009). Achieve Cultural Competency. *Training (Minneapolis, Minn.), (February 2009, Vol.46, No.2, p16-17)*. Retrieved from: UMW Library Resources (Business Full Text), December 10, 2009.

Feldt, Liv Egholm & Jakobsen, Michael. (February 2009). Preparing for a global encounter: from: internationalization en route towards globalization, *ACM, (Feb2009, IWIC '09: Proceeding of the 2009 international workshop on Intercultural collaboration)*. Retrieved from: UMW Library Resources (The ACM Digital Library), December 08, 2009.

Heckman, Lucy.(2004). Cultural Intelligence: People Skills for Global Business (Book). *Library Journal, (6/1/2004, Vol. 129 Issue 10, p151-151, 1/5p)*. Retrieved from: UMW Library Resources (Academic Search Complete), December 08, 2009.

Holmes, Andrew. (2002). Intelligent about culture, *Computer Weekly (10/3/2002, p40, 1/2p)*. Retrieved from: UMW Library Resources (Computers & Applied Sciences Complete), December 08, 2009.

Industry Week. (2009). Are You Cued in to Cultural Intelligence? *Industry Week (Nov2009, Vol. 258 Issue 11, p24-24, 1/2p)*. Retrieved from: UMW Library Resources (Academic Search Complete), December 08, 2009.

Joo-seng Tan. (2004). Cultural Intelligence and the Global Economy. *Leadership in Action, (Nov2004, Vol. 24 Issue 5, p19-21, 3p)*. Retrieved from: UMW Library Resources (Academic Search Complete), December 08, 2009.

Koh, Christine; Joseph, Damien; Ang, Soon. (February 2009). Cultural intelligence and collaborative work: intercultural competencies in global technology work teams, *ACM, (Feb2009, IWIC '09: Proceeding of the 2009 international workshop on Intercultural collaboration)*. Retrieved from: UMW Library Resources (The ACM Digital Library), December 08, 2009.

Kumar, Naresh; Rose, Raduan Che.(2008). The Effects of Personality and Cultural Intelligence on International Assignment Effectiveness: A Review. *Journal of Social Sciences (15493652), (2008, Vol. 4 Issue 4, p320-328, 9p)*. Retrieved from: UMW Library Resources (Academic Search Complete), December 08, 2009.

Li-Rong Lilly Cheng. (2007). Cultural Intelligence (CQ), *Communication Disorders Quarterly, (Nov2007, Vol. 29 Issue 1, p36-42, 7p)*. Retrieved from: UMW Library Resources (Academic Search Complete), December 08, 2009.

Messarra, Leila; Karkoulian, Silva; Younes, Aida. (2008). FOUR FACETS OF CULTURAL INTELLIGENCE PREDICTORS OF KNOWLEDGE SHARING INTENTIONS, Review of Business Research, *(2008, Vol. 8 Issue 5, p126-131, 6p)*. Retrieved from: UMW Library Resources (Business Source Complete), December 11, 2009.

Peltokorpi, Vesa & Schneider, Susan C. (February 2009). Communicating across cultures: the interaction of cultural and language proficiency, *ACM, (Feb2009, IWIC '09: Proceeding of the 2009 international workshop on Intercultural collaboration)*. Retrieved from: UMW Library Resources (The ACM Digital Library), December 08, 2009.

Plum, Elisabeth. (February 2004). Cultural intelligence: the art of leading cultural complexity, Association for Computing Machinery (February 2009, p293-296, 3p). Retrieved from: UMW Library Resources (The ACM Digital Library), March 21, 2009.

Publishers Weekly. (2008). Cultural Intelligence: Improving Your CQ to Engage Our Multicultural World. *Publishers Weekly, (12/15/2008, Vol. 255 Issue 50, p50-50, 1/6p)*. Retrieved from: UMW Library Resources (Academic Search Complete), December 08, 2009.

Rabotin, M. (2009). Reading the World: Acquiring Cultural Synergetic Intelligence in Today's Global Economy. *T+D, (February 2009, Vol. 63, no.2, p. 40-3)*. Retrieved from: UMW Library Resources (Business Full Text), December 10, 2009.

Sawhney, Teenna. (Dec. 2008). Cultural Intelligence and Business Behavior, *ICFAI Journal of Soft Skills, (Dec2008, Vol. 2 Issue 4, p31-37, 7p)*. Retrieved from: UMW Library Resources (Business Source Complete), December 11, 2009.

Swami, Viren; Furnham, Adrian; Maakip, Ismail; Ahmad, Mohd Sharani; Nawi, Nurul Hudani Mohd; Voo, Peter S. K.; Christopher, Andrew N.; Garwood, Jeanette . (March 2008). Beliefs about the meaning and measurement of intelligence: a cross-cultural comparison of American, British and Malaysian undergraduates, *Applied Cognitive Psychology (Mar2008, Vol. 22 Issue 2, p235-246)*. Retrieved from: UMW Library Resources (Academic Search Complete), December 08, 2009.

Vance, Charles M., Yongsun, Paik. (2006). Managing a Global Workforce. M.E. Sharpe, Inc.

Wilson, Jill. (2007). Developing a global outlook: Cultural Intelligence. *Ethos, (Dec2007, Vol. 15 Issue 4, p24-25, 2p).* Retrieved from: UMW Library Resources (Academic Search Complete), December 08, 2009.

ABOUT THE AUTHOR

It all started with SOC-201 at Virginia Highlands Community College. This is where Todd became fascinated with applying concepts from sociology and psychology to management and information technology projects. During his second year of college he wrote (not published) his own management framework based on several well-known behavioral concepts. He continued to gravitate in this direction during his graduate work as can be seen with this research project. Todd says that he has learned a lot over the years about the role sociology plays in a work environment, and how human nature can be used to steer a project in a positive direction. However, he still feels as if he hasn't even scratched the surface. Don't be surprised if you eventually see more publications from him on these topics.

As for his educational qualifications, he has a Master's Degree in Management Information Systems from the University of Mary Washington, a Bachelor's in Industrial Technology from Old Dominion University, and two Associate's Degrees from Virginia Highlands Community College. In terms of other credentials, he also has his Security + and CISSP certifications.

He can be found on LinkedIn at:
http://www.linkedin.com/in/tlowdermilk

…and welcomes any questions and feedback…